A Life That Feels Like Living

Elle Bean

A Life That Feels Like Living

ISBN: 979-8-234-02473-2

Published by URDYN Publishing House

Raleigh, NC

First Edition, 2026

United States

For the woman I was when surviving was the only option.
And for the woman I am becoming now.

For Harlow, my daughter, and the life I am learning to live.

For anyone who kept going and still wanted more.

You are allowed to build a life that feels like living.

I was always providing.

I just wasn't arriving.

Table of Contents

I didn't stop working on myself because I gave up.
I stopped because I wanted to live.

For a long time, I believed that if I just worked on myself enough, I would eventually arrive somewhere better.

I read the books. I took the notes. I learned the language. Healing. Growth. Alignment. Becoming. I understood myself deeply. I could explain my patterns. Name my wounds. Trace my reactions back to their origins. I knew where things went wrong and why.

And still, something felt off.

I wasn't broken. I wasn't unaware. I wasn't even unhappy all the time. But I was tired in a way that self-improvement never seemed to touch. Not tired because I wasn't trying hard enough. Tired because I never stopped trying at all.

At some point, without making a formal decision, I stopped working on myself.

Not because I gave up.

Because I noticed what the work was costing me.

I realized I was constantly monitoring my inner world, evaluating my responses, adjusting my behavior, searching for the next version of myself that might finally feel settled. Even rest had become a project. Even joy felt like something I needed to earn or optimize.

I was healing outward, but I wasn't inhabiting my life.

This book didn't come from a breakthrough. It came from a quiet noticing. From realizing that I didn't need to become someone else to feel alive. I needed to stop abandoning myself in the name of improvement.

What changed wasn't my ambition. It was my attention.

I stopped asking, "What's wrong with me?"

I started asking, "What am I missing while I'm trying to fix myself?"

The answer was simple and unsettling.

My life.

This is not a book about self-optimization.

It's not a guide to becoming your best self.

It's not a set of practices meant to make you more productive, regulated, or impressive.

It's a reflection on what happens when you stop postponing presence.

When you stop waiting for clarity before you let a moment count.

When you stop treating your life like a draft.

When you stop believing that ease is something you access only after you've earned it.

A life that feels like living doesn't arrive all at once. It doesn't announce itself. It doesn't require perfection or completion.

It begins when you stay.

Stay with your body.

Stay with your breath.

Stay with the ordinary moments you've been rushing past.

This book is an invitation to notice where you've been moving through your days without fully arriving in them. To consider what might change if you stopped trying to improve your life long enough to actually live it.

There's nothing here you need to become.

Only something you may want to return to.

Chapter One

Always Providing, Never Arriving

I learned how to carry life before I learned how to arrive inside it.

I don't remember a moment when life slowed down
and asked me how I was doing.
It was always moving. Packing. Driving. Adjusting.
Figuring it out.

Some of my earliest memories carry joy and fear at the
same time. Long drives to Las Vegas to help my great-
grandmother, the hum of the road stretching out ahead
of us. Hotel rooms. Arcades glowing with neon lights.
Weekends with my dad at flea markets, the smell of dust
and food in the air, riding horses, dancing with my
cousins like nothing bad could touch us.

It was fun.
And it was fragile.

Because somewhere in the background, things were
already falling apart. My dad disappeared. My mom was
sick in ways I didn't yet know how to name. And one
day, without ceremony, our life shifted. We became
wards of the court. Children in motion. Children
learning early that nothing was guaranteed.

We were lucky. My grandmother took us in. She became
our safety net. Not the kind of safety that erases fear,
but the kind that shows up anyway. She worked. She
taught us how to help. How to be useful. How to keep
going even when life wasn't fair. Compassion wasn't
something she talked about. It was something she lived.

What I learned early wasn't how to build wealth.
It was how to survive.

Money meant getting through, not getting ahead. Safety felt temporary. Borrowed. Something you could lose at any moment. Home wasn't just a place. It was a wish.

Before I was eight, I slept in a car, wrapped in blankets. I remember walking to a shelter, bags packed, waiting for rides. On days when food showed up, we were grateful. But what I wanted more than anything was a home. Somewhere you didn't have to stay ready to leave.

That's why home still matters so much to me.
Home means exhaling.

Even as an adult, stability came late. Couches. Floors. Roommates. Seasons of working just to keep a rental car so I had somewhere to sleep. And still, I lived. I laughed. I found joy where I could. Survival didn't cancel joy. It just made it quieter.

When I finally got my own place, one I had watched being built and told myself I would live in, something shifted. I had manifested before, not always what I wanted, but what I needed. This felt like proof. Not that life was easy, but that I was capable.

Still, something didn't settle.

Stability brought relief, but it also came with pressure. Financial weight. Responsibility. A constant hum of providing. I became efficient. Strong. Composed. Somewhere along the way, strength turned into emotional containment. Cry if you need to. Wipe your tears. Keep moving.

That sentence lived in my body long before I ever said it out loud.

Then motherhood arrived.

Motherhood didn't disrupt my life. It magnified it. Fight-or-flight stopped being a phase and became a setting. Autopilot felt necessary. Because now it wasn't just about me. Failure wasn't an option. Rest felt negotiable. Presence felt earned instead of assumed.

I loved my child deeply. And still, there were moments when I wasn't present. Overtime hours. Side dreams. Exhaustion that sat heavy in my body. During my pregnancy, I lost my best friend, a platonic soulmate who had known me in ways few people ever had. That loss hardened something in me. It reminded me how quickly people can disappear.

Carry it yourself, I told myself again.

Work took more than time. It took energy. It took softness. It took my mornings. I woke up providing, not arriving. Chasing stability instead of living inside it. I kept telling myself later. Later I'll slow down. Later I'll enjoy it. Later I'll live.

Later never came.

What started to ache wasn't my life on paper. It was my life in my body. I wasn't ungrateful. I was tired. Tired of surviving so well that no one noticed I was still surviving.

I had become very good at holding everything together. At being the one others could rely on. At creating safety, solutions, continuity. But I had no language for what it cost me to never arrive anywhere myself.

I was always providing.
I was never landing.

One day, I stopped consuming all the advice and asked myself a quieter question.

What does a life that feels like living actually look like?

Not a dream life. Not a future version of me.
An ordinary Tuesday.
A slow morning.
A cup of coffee or tea.
Stretching. Breathing.

Time with my child.
Ease in my own space.

I didn't want escape.
I wanted arrival.

And maybe the truest thing I can say about my life so far is this: while life has had many ups and downs, I have always shown up authentically. I may have lost the vision a time or two, but I always found my way back to myself.

Reflect and Pour

What does a life that feels like living actually look like?

Chapter Two

The Chase

Movement kept me alive.
Stillness asked me who I was without momentum.

For a long time, I thought movement meant progress.

If I was busy, I was doing something right.

If I was tired, it meant I was working hard enough.

If I was overwhelmed, I told myself that was just the cost of being responsible.

I learned early how to chase. Chase stability. Chase security. Chase the version of life that looked like it would finally let me breathe. I didn't call it hustling then. It was just survival with better clothes and a calendar full of obligations.

Somewhere along the way, providing became my identity.

I was good at it too. I showed up. I worked hard. I figured things out. I moved from temporary to permanent, from barely holding on to promotions, raises, better addresses. On paper, it looked like forward motion. Growth. Progress.

But internally, I was always arriving late to myself.

Autopilot became my default setting. Wake up. Get through the day. Handle what needed handling. Repeat. I told myself this was what adulthood looked like. Especially motherhood. Especially responsibility. Especially being the one who couldn't afford to fall apart.

I didn't feel miserable all the time. That's the part people don't talk about. *You can be functional and still feel disconnected.* You can be grateful and still feel empty. I laughed. I joked. I showed up as the version of myself people expected. The capable one. The light one. The one who always seemed to be doing well.

But my nervous system never got the memo that we were safe.

Fight or flight stayed switched on. Always scanning. Always preparing for the other shoe to drop. That's what years of instability teach you. Even when things look okay, you stay ready.

Work fed that instinct perfectly.

Work gave me structure. Deadlines. A reason to stay in motion. A place to pour my energy so I didn't have to sit too long with my thoughts. And when motherhood layered on top of that, the chase intensified. Now there was more to protect. More to maintain. More at stake.

I told myself I didn't have time to slow down.

I told myself rest was irresponsible.

I told myself I would pause when things felt more secure.

But secure kept moving.

The truth is, I didn't just chase stability. I chased permission. Permission to enjoy my life without guilt. Permission to want more than survival. Permission to stop proving how strong I was.

I chased external markers because internally, I still didn't trust ease.

Slow mornings felt indulgent. Stillness felt unsafe. If I wasn't doing something productive, I felt behind. Even joy had to be justified.

Had to be earned.

Had to fit neatly into the margins of a busy life.

And yet, my body kept trying to tell me something.

The exhaustion that sleep didn't fix.

The tightness in my chest when nothing was technically wrong.

The moments when I stared out a window or sat in a coffee shop and felt a quiet longing I couldn't name.

Motherhood made the cracks harder to ignore.

I wanted my child to feel safe. Present. Seen. I wanted to give her the home I never had. The softness I had to grow into later. But how do you teach presence when you're always rushing? How do you model ease when your nervous system only understands urgency?

Some days I looked at my life and felt proud. Other days I felt like I was sprinting on a treadmill that never stopped.

Always providing.

Never arriving.

The chase didn't make me a bad person. It made me a capable one. A responsible one. A reliable one. But it also kept me distant from myself. From my body. From the version of life I actually wanted to live.

I didn't need another promotion.

I didn't need another productivity hack.

I didn't need another plan.

What I needed was permission to stop chasing long enough to ask a different question.

Not how do I keep up?

But what am I running toward, and why?

That question didn't change my life overnight.

But it cracked something open.

And once you notice you're running, you can't unsee it.

Reflect and Pour

Does movement equate to progress?

Is providing your identity?

What are you working towards and why?

What is your definition of joy?

Are you worthy of joy?

Chapter Three

The Pause

The body whispers before it screams.
I had been ignoring the whispers.

The pause did not arrive as relief.

It arrived as discomfort.

There was no dramatic breaking point. No collapse. No moment where everything fell apart and forced me to stop. My life looked fine from the outside. I was functioning. Showing up. Taking care of what needed to be taken care of.

But inside, something was tightening.

I noticed it in my body before I understood it in my mind. A constant bracing. A readiness I could not turn off. Even during moments that were supposed to be calm, my nervous system stayed alert, as if something was about to happen.

I had become very good at reading myself. Too good.

I could track my reactions in real time. Name my triggers. Adjust my tone. Redirect my thoughts. I knew exactly what I was feeling and why. I had language for everything.

What I didn't have was rest.

At some point, I realized I was never fully inside my experience. I was always standing slightly outside of it, observing, correcting, improving. Even moments of joy came with commentary. Even stillness felt like something I needed to justify.

The pause came when I noticed how much effort it took to keep managing myself.

Not fixing myself. Managing.

I wasn't falling apart. I was holding together too tightly.

The pause was not intentional at first. It happened in small ways. Sitting longer than usual in the car before going inside. Letting the dishes wait. Staring out a window without reaching for my phone. These moments felt strange, almost unsafe, like I was doing something wrong.

My instinct was to fill the space. To make the pause useful. To turn it into reflection or insight or growth.

Instead, I let it stay empty.

That was harder than doing anything at all.

Without constant motion, feelings surfaced that I had been neatly organizing and moving past. Fatigue that sleep did not fix. Sadness that did not need an explanation. A grief that was not attached to one specific loss, but to years of moving through life without ever fully landing in it.

I had spent so much time working on myself that I had stopped being with myself.

The pause showed me how deeply I associated worth with effort. If I wasn't improving, I felt stagnant. If I wasn't learning, I felt behind. If I wasn't striving, I felt irresponsible.

Stillness felt like failure.

But the pause was not asking me to quit my life. It was asking me to stop narrating it.

To let moments exist without immediately turning them into meaning. To feel something without rushing to understand it. To trust that awareness did not require constant analysis.

The pause taught me that my nervous system did not need more insight. It needed safety.

Safety came not from answers, but from consistency. From allowing my body to experience moments without urgency. From proving to myself, slowly, that nothing bad would happen if I stopped trying to stay ahead of my own life.

I noticed how often I treated rest as something to recover from. How quickly I reached for distraction when things went quiet. How unfamiliar it felt to simply sit inside a moment without reaching for the next one.

The pause did not make me peaceful overnight.

It made me honest.

Honest about how tired I was. Honest about how much pressure I carried. Honest about how often I confused self-awareness with self-surveillance.

In the pause, I began to see that healing does not always require more effort. Sometimes it requires less interference.

Less fixing.

Less monitoring.

Less trying to arrive somewhere else.

The pause did not give me answers.

It gave me space.

And in that space, I realized something simple and unsettling.

I did not need to become someone new.

I needed to stop leaving myself every time things slowed down.

Reflect and Pour

How often do you let moments exist without immediately turning them into meaning, rushing to understand it, or requiring constant analysis?

Does stillness feel like failure?

Chapter Four

Becoming

Strength was my currency.
Resilience was my reputation.

Becoming was never about adding more.

For most of my life, I thought it was. More insight. More strength. More proof that I was evolving. Becoming sounded active, ambitious, forward moving. It felt like something you earned by enduring enough and learning the right lessons along the way.

But what I began to understand was this:

For most of my life, I had been defined by what I could carry.

How much I could handle.

How well I could adapt.

Strength was my currency.

Resilience was my reputation.

But becoming asked a different question.

Not how much can you hold, but what are you still holding that no longer belongs to you?

I had spent so long being a vessel for others that I forgot I was allowed to pour back into myself. I knew how to hold space. How to show up. How to support. I had become fluent in healing outward.

What I hadn't learned was how to receive.

Becoming didn't arrive as confidence. It arrived as exposure. As moments where I could no longer rely on competence alone to carry me through. It showed up in the quiet spaces where productivity wasn't available to hide behind.

Motherhood made this impossible to ignore.

In raising my daughter, I saw myself reflected back to me in real time. My impatience. My tenderness. My exhaustion. My joy. My love for life. All of it mirrored without judgment. I could see where my nervous system tightened. Where my tone sharpened. Where my presence drifted.

And I could also see something else.

My capacity for delight.

My instinct to sing and dance in the kitchen.

My ability to laugh in the middle of an ordinary day.

Becoming wasn't about correcting myself for her sake. It was about recognizing that she was watching how I lived inside my life. Not just what I said, but how I moved. How I rested. How I returned to myself after hard moments.

There were days we danced around the living room to whatever song was playing. Ed Sheeran. Olivia Dean. Sometimes Clipse— "Birds Don't Sing," a song my daughter loves. Music filled the space, and for a few minutes, nothing else mattered. Not what was unfinished. Not what was waiting. Just the moment we were in.

Those moments mattered more than I realized.

They reminded me that becoming wasn't happening somewhere ahead of me. It was happening right there. In the choosing of presence over performance. In allowing joy without justification. In letting softness exist alongside responsibility.

I began to notice how often I had confused

being needed with being whole.

Becoming asked me to separate the two.

I did not need to be constantly useful to be worthy. I did not need to exhaust myself to prove my value. I did not need to carry everything to belong to my life.

The wounded healer in me had been busy tending to everyone else. Becoming asked me to turn that care inward without apology.

This did not make me less capable. It made me more honest.

I stopped measuring my growth by how much I could endure. I started measuring it by how present I could remain. How quickly I could soften instead of brace. How gently I could return to myself when I noticed I had disappeared again.

Becoming did not require a new identity.

It required a release.

A release of the belief that strength had to be visible to be real. A release of the story that my value lived in my output. A release of the version of myself who believed rest was something she had to earn.

Becoming was not a destination.

It was a permission.

Permission to be more than what I could carry.

Permission to let joy interrupt the day.

Permission to live without constantly proving that I deserved to be here.

And once I stopped trying to become someone else, something unexpected happened.

I began to recognize myself.

32

Reflect and Pour

Are you defined by how well you adapt? How much you can handle? How strong you are?

Are you capable of receiving? Why or why not?

Chapter Five

Choice

I didn't need a new life.
I needed to choose myself inside the one I already had.

Choice did not arrive loudly.

It did not feel like empowerment or confidence or certainty. It felt quieter than that. More internal. Less dramatic. It showed up as a subtle shift in how I responded to my own life.

For a long time, I believed my life was shaped mostly by circumstance. By what I had to do. By what was required of me. By the responsibilities I carried and the realities I could not ignore. Choice felt like a luxury. Something other people had more access to than I did.

Survival does that. It narrows the field. It teaches you to focus on what is necessary, not what is possible.

But once the pause created space, and becoming loosened its grip, something new became visible.

I had more choice than I thought.

Not the kind of choice that erases responsibility or difficulty. The quieter kind. The kind that lives in small moments. The kind that changes how you move through what is already there.

I could choose how I entered a room.

I could choose whether I stayed tense or softened when nothing was wrong.

I could choose to listen to my body instead of overriding it.

These were not life-altering decisions on paper. But they changed my internal experience of living.

For most of my life, my choices were shaped by fear. Fear of instability. Fear of being unprepared. Fear of things falling apart if I relax too much. That fear made me capable, but it also made me rigid. It kept me braced even when there was no immediate threat.

Choice asked me to notice that.

To notice when I was responding from habit instead of intention.

To notice when urgency was learned, not necessary.

To notice when I was moving quickly because stillness felt unfamiliar.

I began to understand that choice does not always look like action.

Sometimes it looks like restraint.

Not answering right away.

Not fixing something that does not need fixing.

Not filling silence just to avoid discomfort.

Choice showed up when I allowed myself to say no without justification. When I let myself rest without turning it into recovery. When I chose presence over productivity, even for a few minutes.

These choices felt uncomfortable at first. They went against the identity I had built around being reliable, strong, and endlessly capable. They required me to tolerate the feeling of not doing enough, even when I was doing exactly what I needed.

Choice also meant accepting that I could not control everything.

I could not guarantee outcomes. I could not protect myself or my child from every possible pain. I could not plan my way into certainty.

But I could choose how I met the uncertainty.

I could choose to stay connected to myself instead of abandoning my body the moment things felt unclear. I could choose to remain present even when answers were not immediately available.

That was a different kind of power.

Choice shifted my relationship with responsibility. It no longer felt like something was happening to me. It became something I could engage with consciously. I could carry what was mine and set down what was not.

This did not make life easier overnight.

But it made it mine.

Choice taught me that having say in your own life is not about control. It is about participation. About being awake inside your own decisions, even when the options are limited.

Especially when they are limited.

I stopped waiting for permission to live differently. I stopped waiting for the perfect conditions to choose myself. I learned that choice does not require confidence. It requires honesty.

Honesty about what supports me.

Honesty about what drains me.

Honesty about what I can carry and what I no longer need to.

Choice did not give me certainty.

It gave me alignment.

And once I began choosing from that place, something subtle but important changed.

I stopped feeling like my life was happening to me.

I was in it.

Reflect and Pour

What decisions do you make from fear or instability?

What would soften if you allowed yourself to respond instead of reacting?

What is yours to carry? What is not?

If you stopped waiting for perfect conditions, what small choices would you make today?

When was the last time you chose presence over productivity?

Do you choose or survive?

What is the strongest motivation in choosing? Immediate gratification, need, or desire?

Chapter Six

Living

Living didn't arrive as a revelation.
It arrived as permission.

I didn't arrive at living all at once.

There was no clean break between before and after. No dramatic moment where everything slowed and suddenly made sense.

I wasn't burned out in the dramatic way people talk about online. I was worn down in a quieter, more dangerous way.

Still showing up.

Still functioning.

Still doing what needed to be done.

But slowly losing the ability to feel myself inside my own life.

That kind of exhaustion is easy to miss because it looks like responsibility. It looks like strength. It looks like someone who can handle a lot.

I had been handling a lot for a long time.

Living didn't come to me as a revelation. It came as a practice. As something small and almost unremarkable. The kind of thing you could overlook if you were still waiting for permission to rest.

It showed up in the kitchen one morning, standing barefoot on cold tile while something simple cooked on the stove. Music playing low. My daughter moving through the room, half dancing, half humming. Nothing urgent pulling at me. No one needing anything in that exact moment. Just the quiet realization that I was present for it.

I didn't reach for my phone.

I didn't rush the moment along.

I let it be what it was.

For most of my life, living felt conditional. Something I would get to later. Something that would begin once the pressure eased or the money stabilized or the fear finally loosened its grip. I treated my life like a holding pattern. Useful, productive, but temporary.

I see now how often I left myself behind while trying to build something better.

Living didn't mean I stopped wanting more. It didn't mean I stopped striving or planning or imagining a different future. It meant I stopped disappearing while I did those things.

There were still days my body felt tight and braced. Still moments when my chest held that familiar, quiet panic.

Still times I pushed through instead of pausing. But I started noticing sooner. Listening earlier. Interrupting the spiral before it became my baseline.

I began to understand how much my body had been carrying without my consent.

How often I ignored the signals.

How easily I normalized tension.

How quickly I dismissed fatigue as weakness.

Living asked me to slow down enough to hear what I had been overriding.

Not to fix it.

Not to optimize it.

Just to acknowledge it.

Some days, living looked like movement. Stretching in the living room. Taking a walk without turning it into a goal. Letting my body release what it had been holding all day.

Some days, it looked like creativity. Coloring beside my daughter. Baking something that didn't need to be perfect. Letting my hands do something without asking what it would become.

Some days, it was sound. Music filling the room. Singing too loudly. Dancing badly. Laughing in the middle of the kitchen for no reason other than the fact that we could.

These moments didn't solve anything. They didn't change my circumstances overnight. But they softened

the edges. They reminded me that my life wasn't only made of effort and endurance.

I was still allowed to enjoy it.

The hardest part of living wasn't making time for it. It was trusting that I deserved to feel okay before everything was figured out. Letting myself experience ease without waiting for permission. Allowing presence to coexist with ambition.

I had spent so long believing that relief came after survival. That rest was something earned only once the work was done. Living challenged that belief quietly, persistently, until I could no longer ignore it.

A life doesn't need to be extraordinary to feel real.

It needs to be inhabited.

Living wasn't the reward at the end of the journey.

It was the practice that made the journey bearable.

And slowly, almost without noticing, I stopped waiting for my life to begin.

I was already in it.

Reflect and Pour

When was the last time you felt present in an ordinary moment?

Do you treat living as something that will begin later?

What warning signals has your body been sending that you've normalized?

What does relaxation look and feel like to you?

Do you need to be exhausted or told to rest?

Chapter Seven

Staying

Leaving was easy.
Staying required trust.

Leaving was never my problem.

I knew how to exit. How to reset. How to start over when things felt heavy or disappointing or uncertain. Movement came naturally to me. It always had. Change felt familiar. Sometimes even comforting.

Staying was different.

Staying asked for something I hadn't practiced much before. Not endurance. Not resilience. Not strength.

Staying asked for presence.

For patience.

For the willingness to remain inside a moment without rushing to fix it or flee from it.

For most of my life, I believed movement meant progress. If something felt off, I changed it. If a version of my life became uncomfortable, I outgrew it. That instinct served me well in survival. It helped me adapt. It kept me moving forward when standing still was not an option.

But it also taught me to leave myself the moment things slowed down.

Staying is not passive. It is not settling. It is not giving up. *Staying is an active decision to remain in relationship with your life even when it does not look the way you imagined it would.*

There were seasons when staying felt unbearable. When every part of me wanted relief, escape, clarity. When I wanted answers instead of process. Resolution instead of uncertainty.

But staying asked me to sit with the in between.

To stay with body sensations I usually pushed past.

To stay with emotions I preferred to intellectualize.

To stay with a version of myself that did not yet feel finished or confident or complete.

I had to learn the difference between intuition and avoidance.

Leaving often felt like clarity.

Staying felt like confusion.

But confusion is not always a signal to go. Sometimes it is a sign that something is still unfolding.

Staying meant continuing with the small practices that grounded me even when they stopped feeling exciting. It meant showing up to routines that no longer offered immediate relief or visible progress. It meant trusting repetition over urgency.

There were days staying looked quiet and unimpressive. Making the same meals. Having the same conversations. Carrying the same responsibilities without recognition or applause. No dramatic shift. No moment of arrival.

Just continuity.

And continuity is where many people leave.

Staying also meant staying with myself emotionally. Not rushing to reframe pain before it had been fully felt. Not turning disappointment into motivation too quickly. Letting sadness exist without extracting meaning from it right away.

That was uncomfortable.

I preferred insight. Movement. Understanding.

But staying taught me that some truths only surface when you stop trying to outthink your experience.

The nervous system does not respond to urgency. It responds to safety. And safety is built through predictability and trust. Through staying long enough for the body to believe it is not about to be abandoned again.

Staying was how I stopped living in constant preparation mode. Always bracing. Always anticipating

the next shift. Always waiting for something to fall apart.

I began to understand that stability is not the absence of change. It is the presence of support. Internal and external.

And support requires staying long enough to receive it.

There were moments when staying felt like failure. When nothing seemed to be moving fast enough. When I questioned whether I was wasting time. When I wondered if I should be doing more, becoming more, pushing harder.

But staying reminded me that not every season is meant for acceleration.

Some seasons are meant for integration.

For learning how to live inside what you have already built.

For proving to yourself that you can remain steady without constant upheaval.

For letting your body catch up to your life.

I did not stay because it was easy.

I stayed because I needed to learn how.

And once I did, I realized something important.

The life I was searching for did not require another beginning.

It required my presence where I already was.

Reflect and Pour

What does leaving look like to you?

What feelings do you rush to reframe before you feel them?

What are you afraid will happen if you stay?

What does a reset look like to you?

Chapter Eight

Returning

I didn't need to reinvent myself.
I needed to come back.

Returning was not a dramatic homecoming.

There was no single moment where everything clicked and stayed that way. No permanent arrival. Returning happened again and again, often quietly, often without ceremony.

At first, I thought returning meant going back. Back to a version of myself that felt more grounded. More alive. Less tired. I treated it like recovery. Like something I needed to do after drifting too far from center.

I misunderstood it.

Returning was not about reclaiming a past self. It was about learning how to come back to the present one.

I noticed how often I left without realizing it. How quickly my attention drifted ahead to what needed to be done, what needed to be solved, what might go wrong next. My body stayed in the room, but my mind moved on without me.

Returning began as a gentle interruption.

A breath I noticed halfway through holding.

A tension in my shoulders I hadn't realized I was carrying.

A moment where I caught myself rushing through something that didn't need to be rushed.

These moments were small, but they mattered.

For most of my life, I had treated disconnection as failure. If I drifted, I judged myself. If I lost presence, I spiraled into self-correction. I thought awareness meant staying centered at all times.

Returning taught me something kinder.

Leaving is human. Returning is the practice.

I began to understand that the work was not staying perfectly present. It was noticing when I wasn't and coming back without punishment.

That changed everything.

I stopped narrating my missteps as proof that I was doing something wrong. I stopped treating distraction as a personal flaw. I learned to return the same way I would guide my child back to safety. Calmly. Without shame. Without urgency.

Returning softened my relationship with myself.

It reminded me that presence is not a state you achieve once and maintain forever. It is a rhythm. A movement in and out. A willingness to come back again when you notice you've left.

Some days returning looked like sitting quietly after a hard moment instead of rushing to recover. Some days it looked like naming what I was feeling instead of pushing past it. Some days it looked like doing nothing at all.

There were times I returned in tears. Crying in the closet or the shower so my child would not see me sad. Wiping my face before stepping back into the room. Trying to carry joy even when I felt heavy.

I thought I was protecting her.

What I was really learning was how deeply I believed I had to hold everything together.

Returning asked me to soften that belief. To let myself feel without immediately containing it. To trust that presence did not require performance.

The more I practiced returning, the less distance I traveled when I drifted. The gap between disconnection and awareness grew smaller. The return grew gentler.

I stopped fearing the moments I lost myself.

I trusted that I knew how to come back.

Returning did not make me immune to stress or grief or exhaustion. It gave me a way through them. A way to meet myself again without starting over.

I learned that I did not need to rebuild my life every time I felt lost.

I needed to return to it.

And the more often I did, the more familiar home became.

Reflect and Pour

What is your definition of emotional intelligence?

How does emotional intelligence show up in your daily life?

When emotions rise, how do you usually respond?

What might change if you responded with more awareness?

How do you define being present?

How often are you present? Why or why not?

Chapter Nine

Wanting More

Wanting more was never about excess.
It was about breath.

For a long time, I told myself I should be grateful and leave it at that.

Gratitude became a way to quiet desire. A way to soften the ache without ever addressing it. I learned how to be thankful and tired at the same time. How to say I was fine while feeling stretched thin underneath it all.

Wanting more felt dangerous.

Like a betrayal of my past.

Like proof that I had not healed enough.

Like evidence that I was ungrateful for what I already had.

I absorbed the message that contentment meant acceptance, and acceptance meant silence. That if I had survived, I should not ask for ease. That if I was doing better than before, I should not want anything else.

But the truth is, wanting more was never about excess.

It was about breath.

It came from memory. From knowing what it feels like to live without margin. To count every dollar. To carry responsibility without relief. To be one unexpected expense away from panic. My nervous system remembers that life even when my circumstances change.

So when I say I want more, what I am really saying is this:

I want safety that lasts.

I want stability that does not require constant vigilance.

I want a life that supports my body instead of draining it.

Money, for me, has never been about luxury. It has been about exhale. About waking up without dread. About time that is not already claimed. About being present with my child without my mind calculating what is due next.

For a long time, I downplayed that desire. I thought wanting money made me shallow or unspiritual. I thought it meant I had not learned the lesson yet.

But wanting more does not mean I am dissatisfied with my life.

It means I am committed to staying in it.

I do not want more so I can escape.

I want more so I can remain.

I also want beauty. Space that feels intentional. Days that are not only obligation. I want time to create, to wander, to linger without guilt. I want softness without scarcity sitting underneath it.

For a long time, I believed I had to choose between presence and ambition. Between peace and desire. Between living slowly and wanting more.

That was a false choice.

Wanting more does not pull me out of presence anymore. It clarifies it. It shows me what kind of life I am trying to sustain. What pace I need. What structures support me. What quietly depletes me.

I no longer shame myself for wanting a life that feels spacious. Or for imagining ease. Or for wanting enough money that my nervous system can finally rest.

I do not apologize for wanting access. To time. To healthcare. To travel. To opportunity. To options.

I want my child to grow up seeing that ease is possible. That joy does not have to be earned through exhaustion. That success can look like presence, not constant striving.

Wanting more does not erase gratitude.

It deepens it.

Because when I am not constantly worried about survival, I have more capacity to notice what is already here. I participate instead of endure. I enjoy instead of brace.

I am no longer interested in romanticizing struggle. I have done enough of that already. Struggle taught me resilience. But resilience alone is not a life.

I want sustainability.

I want a life where ambition does not cost me my body. Where joy does not feel borrowed. Where rest is not something I have to recover from.

Wanting more is not me reaching beyond myself.

It is me listening.

Listening to what my body needs.

Listening to what my nervous system has been asking for quietly.

Listening to the truth that peace without provision is fragile.

I am allowed to want a life that holds me.

I am allowed to want enough.

And wanting more, I have learned, does not mean I am ungrateful.

It means I am honest.

Reflect and Pour

Are there areas in your life; physically or emotionally where you want more?

Do you feel worthy? Why or why not?

Do you find yourself wanting more when it comes to things or personal growth/Personal development? Why?

Were you ever taught that wanting more was selfish, ungrateful, or unrealistic? How did that shape you?

Chapter Ten

Enough

Enough isn't a limit.
It's a season.

Enough did not arrive as certainty.

It arrived as a loosening.

Not the kind that comes with having everything figured out, but the kind that happens when you stop gripping your life so tightly. When you realize, you do not need to keep proving that you are allowed to be here.

For a long time, enough felt like a threat. Like a signal to stop wanting. Like a word that meant shrinking or settling or giving up on the life I imagined. I resisted it because I thought it asked me to quiet my desire.

It did not.

Enough asked me to quiet the fight.

The fight to stay ahead.

The fight to justify my rest.

The fight to become something else before I could feel okay.

Enough was not a finish line. It was a state of honesty.

Honesty about what this season could hold.

Honesty about what I had already built.

Honesty about what my body needed now.

I had spent years moving as if my life was always about to start. Preparing. Planning. Enduring. Waiting for the moment when things would finally feel stable enough to enjoy. Enough invited me to stop postponing my presence.

It asked me to notice what was already here.

A roof that felt like mine.

A rhythm that no longer demanded constant urgency.

Moments of connection that did not need to be earned.

Enough did not mean I stopped wanting more. It meant I stopped measuring my worth by how much I was chasing. It meant I allowed myself to feel grounded even while holding future dreams.

Enough created space inside my body.

Space to breathe without bracing.

Space to rest without guilt.

Space to feel joy without scanning for what might go wrong next.

There were days I did not feel fully at ease. Days where fear still whispered. Days where my mind returned to old patterns. Enough did not erase those moments. It softened my response to them.

I no longer treated discomfort as a sign that something was wrong. I recognized it as part of being alive.

Enough taught me that peace is not the absence of desire. It is the absence of self-abandonment.

I could want more without leaving myself. I could feel content without closing the door on what might come next. I could live inside my life without waiting for it to become something else first.

Enough was not passive.

It was an active choice to stop postponing my own arrival.

To let ordinary days count.

To trust that stability does not require constant motion.

To believe that I was allowed to inhabit my life as it was unfolding.

Enough did not make me smaller.

It made me present.

And presence, I learned, was what I had been reaching for all along.

Reflect and Pour

How does enough resonate with you?

What does enough mean to you? How does it show up for you?

In what ways have you abandon yourself in the name of progress?

*For anyone still learning
how to live inside their own life.*

A life that feels like living doesn't wait for permission.

I used to think a life that feels like living would announce itself.

That it would arrive all at once, with certainty and proof. That there would be a moment where the struggle quieted, the questions softened, and I could finally say I had arrived. I thought I would recognize it because everything would feel finished.

That is not how it happened.

What I know now is that a life that feels like living does not remove difficulty. It changes how you meet it. It does not eliminate fear. It teaches you how to stay present without letting fear decide everything for you. It does not mean you stop wanting more. It means you stop withholding yourself from the life you are already inside.

A life that feels like living is not dramatic.

It is made of ordinary days that are allowed to count. Of mornings that do not need to be optimized. Of work that exists alongside rest. Of joy that is not earned through exhaustion. Of pauses that do not require permission.

It is a life where you stop waiting to feel worthy of your own presence.

I did not arrive here because I figured everything out. I arrived because I stopped abandoning myself along the way. I learned how to return. How to stay. How to let enough be enough without shrinking my desires or silencing my imagination.

I learned that home is not something you find once and keep forever. It is something you return to, again and again, inside yourself. I learned that living is not a reward for surviving. It is something you are allowed to do at the same time.

This book is not an answer.

It is an invitation.

An invitation to notice where you are rushing past yourself.

An invitation to let this season count.

An invitation to stop postponing joy until everything is resolved.

You do not need to arrive anywhere else to begin living.

You do not need permission to want more.

You do not need perfection to be present.

You do not need to finish becoming to belong to your life.

If there is anything I hope you carry with you from these pages, it is this:

You are allowed to stay.

You are allowed to want.

You are allowed to rest inside the life you are building.

A life that feels like living is not waiting for you somewhere ahead.

It is already here, asking you to notice it.

Ways I Return

These are not rules.

They are not routines I follow perfectly or consistently. They are simply the ways I return to myself when life pulls me away.

I share them gently. Not as instruction, but as companionship. Take what fits. Leave what does not. Let them be reminders, not requirements.

Breathing Before Fixing

When my body feels ahead of my thoughts, I breathe first.

Not to calm myself down.

Not to make anything disappear.

Just to come back into my body long enough to hear what it is asking for.

Sometimes it is three breaths. Sometimes it is one. Sometimes it is a pause at the sink or in the car before I walk inside. Breath reminds me that urgency does not always mean danger.

Slow Mornings When Possible

Not every morning is slow. Some are rushed and loud and full.

But when I can, I protect the first few minutes of the day. Stretching. Quiet. A warm drink. Letting my nervous system wake up without demand.

Slow mornings do not make my life perfect.

They make it inhabitable.

Music as Regulation

Music brings me back faster than almost anything.

Sometimes it is something soft and grounding. Sometimes it is something that makes me laugh, dance, or sing out loud with my child in the living room. Music reminds me that joy does not need to be scheduled. It can interrupt the day and still count.

Small Acts of Creativity

I do not wait to feel inspired.

I cook. I bake. I color. I paint. I rearrange space. I make something small with my hands. Creativity grounds me in the present moment. It reminds me that I am allowed to create without producing anything of value for anyone else.

Naming What I Am Feeling

When I can name what I am feeling, it loosens its grip.

I do not analyze it. I do not fix it. I simply name it. Tired. Overwhelmed. Sad. Hopeful. Restless. Naming brings honesty back into my body. It keeps emotions from hardening into identity.

Letting Ordinary Moments Count

I stop waiting for big moments to feel alive.

I notice the way light comes through the window. The sound of my child laughing. The quiet of the evening. The comfort of sitting without doing anything else.

Ordinary moments are not filler.

They are the substance.

Returning Without Punishment

When I drift, I come back gently.

I do not lecture myself. I do not spiral. I return the same way I would guide my child back to safety. Calmly. Without shame. Without urgency. This has been one of the most healing practices of my life.

Asking What Supports Me Now

Not what should support me.

Not what used to support me.

What supports me now.

Some seasons need structure. Some need softness.
Some need both. I let my practices change as I change.

These are not the things that fixed me.

They are the things that help me stay.

If any of them meet you where you are, let them be
yours.

If not, trust that you already know what brings you
back.

You do not need more discipline to live a life that feels
like living.

You need attention.

You need permission.

You need gentleness.

And you are allowed to begin exactly where you are.

Acknowledgments

Writing this book required honesty, courage, and more quiet reflection than I expected. I am grateful for the people who supported me along the way and held space for this work to exist.

Barra, thank you for always seeing me and believing in my abilities. Your wisdom, encouragement, and your willingness to read this book and decide to see it through with me mean more than I can fully put into words. Thank you for the weekly video chats, the love and support, and even the random gifts—because you understand how life can be as a mom. Even from thousands of miles away, you show up for me in ways that make distance feel small.

Thank you for always seeing me and for being my constant cheerleader. Thank you for pushing me when I needed it most. Your love and support do not go unnoticed. You are beyond a friend. You are my sister.

To my daughter Harlow, thank you for being the reason I learned how to slow down and pay attention to the life happening right in front of me. You remind me every day that joy can be simple, presence is powerful, and that love is the center of everything that matters.

And to the quiet moments that made this book possible. The early mornings, the late nights, the pauses in between responsibilities where reflection found its way onto the page. This book exists because I chose to keep showing up to those moments.

With love and gratitude

Elle

ABOUT THE AUTHOR

Elle Bean is a writer and reflective storyteller whose work explores presence, responsibility, and what it means to live inside a life that is still unfolding. Drawing from lived experience and motherhood, she writes with quiet honesty for readers who are capable, thoughtful, and ready to step out of preparation mode and into the life already happening.

Through essays, reflections, and personal storytelling, Elle's work centers on intentional living, emotional awareness, and the courage to slow down long enough to recognize what truly matters. She lives in North Carolina with her daughter and continues learning how to build a life that feels like living.

You can follow her reflections and everyday moments on YouTube

@livingwellwithelle

www.alifethatfeelslikeliving.com

www.ingramcontent.com/pod-product-compliance
Lightning Source LLC
Chambersburg PA
CBHW051445140726
47987CB00006B/2550